I0470313

Ranch and Farm
Marketing Guide

www.ranchandfarmmarketingguide.com
By Wesley R. Young with Rich Vance

www.ranchandfarmmarketingguide.com
By Wesley R. Young with Rich Vance

Ranch and Farm Marketing Guide

By Wesley R Young
with Rich Vance

Ranch and Farm Marketing Guide

Address all inquires to:

Wesley R Young
PO Box 10
Middleport, OH 45760

www.ranchandfarmmarketingguide.com
info@ ranchandfarmmarketingguide.com

This publication is designed to provide accurate and authoritative information in regard to the subject matter covered. It is sold with the understanding that the author is not engaged in rendering legal, accounting or other professional services.

ISBN 13: 978-1461117469
ISBN 10: 1461117461

www.ranchandfarmmarketingguide.com
By Wesley R. Young with Rich Vance

www.ranchandfarmmarketingguide.com
By Wesley R. Young with Rich Vance

Business Mindset

I decided to open this book with a small chapter on business mindset and follow it up with one on getting started. These two things when combined can help you create a powerful force that can lead you and your business to greater heights than ever imagined.

So many business owners seem to just ride along with the flow of their business without ever doing the things they need to do to improve. Sometimes this comes from a level of comfort they have achieved or from fear of change. But the thing they are often overlooking is that a business is either improving or declining. A business can never just stand still. In order to improve your business you need to start developing the best business mindset that you can. While some of the advice that follows may seem a bit harsh, don't make the mistake of discounting it before taking the time to actually think about what you are reading.

You will read about the importance of the customer in this book, and there is no doubt that the customer is very important, but as a business owner you need to understand that the customer is a means to an end. They are not the focus of your business. Your responsibility as a business owner is to make as much money as possible within your ethical and moral standards for the owner of the business. Often that owner is you or a combination of you and others. By making your business as profitable as possible, you will have the choice as to how you spend your money, how you operate your business and who you can help. You are not in the business of providing jobs or taking care of anyone but you and your family.

While it may not sound correct to many of you, the fact is that the most important thing in your business is the bottom line. How much profit you have left over after all of your expenses is not the only thing of importance in your business, but it is the most important thing. The magic of basing every single decision you make in your business on the bottom line is that it improves every aspect of your business. The reason you offer superior customer service and high quality products is not because it is the right thing to do, but because it is the most profitable way to run your business now and in the future. You don't want to sell inferior products because the customers who buy them won't come back for more. The reason you want to maximize the profit on every item you sell is because it will allow you to expand your business, market in new places and allow new customers the opportunity to use your products and services.

I hope some of the ideas in this book can help you reach your goals in your business. But even if you don't use anything else in this book, if you start thinking about every decision based on how it will affect your bottom line you will instantly start improving your business.

Just Do It, Whatever It Is, Right Now

I have found that the single largest problem that I have with the productivity of my marketing efforts is the same problem that many other marketers have. Because of this, I wanted to share a few thoughts with you in hopes that they may be the final trigger that starts you on your own path to financial freedom through your business.

So what is this big problem? As you may have guessed from the title, the problem is not starting. Most of us can develop ideas that may be profitable, but we often have a hard time getting started. I can only speak from personal experience, but I have what seems like hundreds of ideas about ways to make money through marketing, but out of each 100, I often will only actually do one or two. Some of the ideas get discarded because after looking into them further they turn out to be either bad ideas or would turn such a low profit that they aren't worth the effort, but many of the remaining ones don't get done because they don't get started. Almost every time I actually start something and see it through, I make money at it. Is this because I'm smarter or luckier than you? I seriously doubt it. I would even go so far as to say that most of you are at least as smart as I am, and the fact of the matter is that you don't have to be anywhere near a rocket scientist to make a good living using marketing.

The biggest difference between the winners and losers is so often that the winners take action and the losers do not. I decided to start an online business between two and three years before I actually did. Looking back, if I had started when I first decided to, I would probably be much better off than I am now. That isn't to say that I am not doing well, it is just saying that the results could have been magnified. But probably more importantly, if I had not finally started, I would STILL be working for someone else, getting further and further into debt, and be miserable.

The moral of the story is to take action. If you have wanted to attempt to make more money using marketing but haven't started yet, don't wait another minute. Do it right now. My first web site (actually my first several web sites) sucked. I did just about everything you could think of wrong. But it was the first step towards where I am today, which is working my own schedule from the comfort of my home. In addition, as I learned the mistakes I had made, I fixed that first web site and made a couple thousand dollars from it in the year or so that I owned it. No, a couple thousand dollars isn't a ton of money, but by starting somewhere and learning and not giving up, I progressed to web sites making many times that a month.

Your first step is your most important one. Even reading solid information like this book is somewhat of a first step, so congratulations on that, but take the next step and start your marketing today. Find a few ideas in this book that you think might help you and your business and try them. I urge you to take the first step. You will more than likely be pleased with the results.

The Farmer's Market

The farmer's market has been around for a long time and offers the farmer a great opportunity to interact with the customer. Farmers markets offer a variety of products to the customer all fresh from the farm and represented by the farmer. That is one of the many reasons farmers markets are successful. The personal connection made between the customer and the seller. In any business having a connection with whomever business is being conducted helps to build that relationship for the future. A person who has a personal connection with a business is a much more loyal customer than a person who is purchasing from a retailer they don't know. Lets face it, would you rather help out a friend while buying a product that you need? Or would you prefer to go down to the store where you don't have a personal association and help them instead? In the agriculture industry, customers are very valuable and important to the success of a business, especially those that market directly.

It is important to understand that if you are selling products to the public, you are not only a producer you are also a marketer. Everything you do is in the public eye and how it is perceived reflects on you and your business. How your product is presented, how it is packaged, the type of area you sell from, the type of service the customer receives, the quality of your product, and how you present yourself are all important. These things are what the customer sees when they see your display, web site, products, or you in a professional setting. So it is very important to take that opportunity to do everything to the best of your ability to gain the respect and business of your potential customers. It is the personal selling and relationships that you build with your customers that help add to your success in business.

There are many aspects of selling or when dealing directly with the public. The primary thing we want to focus on at this time is customer relationships. It is just one of many important steps for any business. Raising high quality products is very important and having good price points is also important in business. As with so many markets today things are competitive, so you may not be the only person selling a certain variety of pepper at a farmers market. So let's assume that you and your competitor both have equal quality products at similar price points and that you both have nice displays and packaging. What separates you from your competitor? It is the customer who will make the final decision. So with all things being equal between two retailers what will that final deciding factor be? It might very well come down to you as a person. It goes back to whom do you want to do business with and support, your friend or the person you don't know.

That is why the value of customer relationships becomes important. Sure it is great to sell some products to a customer one time, but the real value is in creating a loyal customer who likes your product that will return time and time again. These are the customers who will make you successful. Having the best quality product you can produce is part of running a good business, but the other part is good customer service and relationships. Just like you want to be treated well when you do business, so do your customers. Everyone likes to walk into an establishment and be recognized. They want to feel important. A customer who feels like he or she is valued has much more loyalty than one who feels unappreciated. They are spending their hard earned money with you, and they want to buy quality products, but also receive good customer service. Things can be made complicated sometimes, or kept really simple. You will see things like this from large companies that become focused only on profit and lose site of something very important, the customer. How many people do you know who have changed product brands or service companies because of a bad experience? Everyone has done this, and why? Because they didn't feel like they were being treated fairly, especially by someone they had no personal connection with.

In today's economy, or in any economy or situation, can you afford to lose a customer who purchases from you on a weekly or monthly basis? Certainly not. That is why you need to understand your customer and develop a relationship to avoid that from happening. How are customers greeted when they approach your area of business? This is where personal selling comes into play, but it is not only the product you are selling it is you! Being friendly and honest with a customer is a good way to start. Take the time to get to know them while you educate them about your product. Everyone likes to be involved and receive attention; therefore they will often show greater interest as well. Create an opportunity to talk with the customers if you can. Ask them about how they like or use your products. You can offer educational tips and information about what you are selling that gets your customer involved. Also take the time to get feedback from your customers, get their opinion about your products, services, and what they need from you. In general, just engaging in conversation can make a customer feel welcome. Being friendly can open a lot of doors, and create new or repeat customers.

So remember that when dealing with customers face to face to work on building those friendships and relationships that will last years to come. People want to belong and feel connected in all walks of life and business is no different. Business is often conducted where we feel we get good quality and also fair pricing. Sometimes it is not about the price so much as it is the service. Are you willing to pay a little more for something if you get better customer service, or you are treated in a certain way?

Most people will pay a little more to be treated promptly, or if they are given attention that makes them feel valued. This is where you can set yourself apart from your competition. Use your personality to win your customers over and remember it is not always about price.

Using the Internet

In today's advanced technological world, every business should own a web site. Establishing a business profile online is an important tool that everyone should recognize. Most customers do research online about products they want to buy. The fastest way to learn and do research today is to use the Internet; thousands of pages of information are at your fingertips. When a consumer is looking for a location to purchase a product, what is the easiest way to find where to buy it? Today's customer is more educated than ever, price compares more often, and bases decisions on research far more than they used to. With the ability to find products anywhere, the web offers a business an opportunity to reach a customer not normally within their reach.

Using traditional methods of advertising is still important; and using the media to promote your business is tried and true. The use of ads in popular magazines, industry specific publication, radio and television are an important avenue to consider. However they reach only a portion of your potential customers. The Internet is open to everyone and allows you to reach farther than some methods of media. Using both tools together allows you to enhance your marketing program. That is why a web site offers value in allowing you to reach more customers, and gives you a platform to go into greater detail about your company, products or services.

Have you ever tried to find out what your competition is doing online? Do they own a web site? How are they using it? Does it give them an advantage over your business? If they are online and you are not, they are certainly touching a market you are not. Let's face it; you are in business to make a profit. If you are not taking full advantage of your potential to generate business you are short changing yourself and company. Everyone wants to save money and increase profits. Using the web can do both for a business. Establishing your business online can increase your visibility, offer new avenues to promote your business, and create a way to stay in contact with your customers.

If you own a web site or are considering one there are some things to look at. What is the definition of a good web site? When you start looking at web sites you will see all sorts of options and styles. There are sites that offer the finest graphics, video, flash applications, lots of photos, combinations of text, pictures, graphic work and pod casts, the possibilities are endless. You may see a simple black and white web site with a plain text header and simple content. Everyone wants the biggest, brightest toys right? Does that mean they are the best tools for the job? How do you know what is best for your business? Your web site needs to look good, but more importantly it must be user friendly.

When people start considering a web site the first thing that comes to mind is cost. Often people just assume that it is too expensive an option to consider; however web site prices vary a lot. You as the customer control what type of site you will have, what it will do, and what it looks like. These are some of the things that affect the cost. Do not assume you cannot afford a web site. It is best to get consultation about your needs and goals to help you determine cost.

When considering whether or not to purchase a web site, it is often helpful to look at it in this way. Web sites are investments that give a return back to the owner. A web site is similar to a piece of real estate. It can be bought, earn income through various methods, and / or help with a specific purpose. The real value is to the owner and what it gives him or her in return. A web site for a business owner usually returns a form of profit. Sometimes these sites are bought and sold like any other product. The values can vary just as the earnings and money invested into the site vary. A good web site should be a valuable part of the marketing machine, used by a business to turn profit, and it should help increase business leads, or sales. Web sites are one of the most cost effective methods of business promotion.

It is easy to fall into the trap of thinking you have to have the biggest and prettiest web site on the Internet. However what will that accomplish for you? It is important to understand the difference between having the best looking sight on the web, and the most effective web site on the web. There are compromises on both sides of course. The key is to get the most effective marketing tool for your business, and your budget. It is important to have a web site that is visually appealing to the customer. It is even more important to have a web site that ranks well in the search engines, functions correctly and obtains business leads or paying customers. Some of the best ranking web sites are often some of the most basic looking web sites, yet they are the most effective. When it comes to investing in a web site, remember what the real goal for your business is.

A web site should represent your business just like you would. You are not only presenting the web site to your customers but to the search engines. If a site is properly built it will rank for common search terms in your industry, thus generating business. A web site improperly built will not effectively rank well with the search engines and then becomes a non-effective marketing tool. A lot of customers have web sites built and have no knowledge of what they really need. A web site can be built by anyone, even a novice. There are thousands of companies building web sites, and a lot of them create beautiful web sites, some create ranking web sites to varying degrees.

It is easy to get lost in the world of web design with so many options to choose from. You start looking and there are all sorts of graphics, text styles, logo designs, backgrounds, and flash applications. While these things are great features, do not overlook the primary purpose of your web site. Generating business is the primary goal. Having a web site that has good traffic going to it allows that to happen. So when you are looking at web site construction consider the search engine optimization experience of the company. There are a lot of companies claiming to S.E.O. sites but many do not truly understand it.

The first step would be to consider what you want a web site to accomplish for your business. Do you want to use it for promotion and a landing page for your customers, are you trying to educate the customer about your products and industry, are you going to sell online? How will customers find your web page? Where will the traffic, come from? What are your goals? It is important to decide what you want to accomplish and how.

First you have to decide do you want natural traffic to the web site? Will you be using other advertising to get traffic to your webpage? Will both methods be used to generate customer contact? This may affect how the web site is built and what it will allow the business to do effectively. Traffic that is driven to the web site from advertising or other methods of promotion know the web address and how to find it because it was provided to them via the ad. For example, you run an ad in an industry publication with your web address. They immediately know how to find you online. That is effective and works for the customer group you are in front of. What if a customer is searching for you online with a search engine? Will they find the web site, where does it rank?

Natural traffic is Internet traffic generated from the search engines. These customers search for phrases, or words, and the search engine brings up pages of related results. So having a web site is more than just building one and putting up graphics and pictures. It has to be search engine friendly to obtain results. There are few unique one of a kind businesses these days so remember you will be competing with other web sites, articles, online magazines, news sources, education sites research material, etc. for search results. It is not the easiest thing to compete with thousands of results. However don't be discouraged, there are specialists who can build good sites that rank for the phrases and terms you want to rank for. That is why it is important to know exactly what your goals for the site are.

A good web site should promote your business in the same way that you would. You want it to be user friendly, not difficult to navigate or hard to use. No one likes to spend a lot of time looking for information or to place an order, especially when there are other companies in the business. It's just like walking into a store; the customer wants good customer service, so the site should offer a good experience for the visitor. Remember that this is just like creating the first impression when you meet someone face to face. Your web site is an extension of your business, thus it should also make a good impression.

The foundation of a good web site is information. This is your opportunity to build a relationship with your customer or potential customer. It should provide quality content that is easy to read and be informative to the reader. This is where you have an opportunity to educate the readers about your business, showcase your products, give them history about the company, information about sales, upcoming products or events and provide contact information. The number of pages needed will depend on your business, products or services, personal preferences and search terms you want to rank for on the search engine. Good content also plays a role in search engine ranking. Quality content is the key to effectively communicating with the customer and building a business relationship.

Visual enhancements are a great companion for good content. The addition of quality pictures, and or video can offer an opportunity to see your products or services, to learn about your company and showcase what you are selling in the most positive manner possible. Having an opportunity for the customer to see things rather than just read about them can help influence their decisions. We are a visual society very accustomed to watching television, so offering a commercial of your product on your web site is no different. The more comfortable and informed a customer becomes the greater the odds of conducting business and creating a lasting professional relationship. Photos can also have S.E.O. value, which will help the site rank better.

The use of social networking sites allows users to follow your business online. They can join your networks and see your latest postings, news updates, information about sales, locations you may be selling or appearing at, or follow along with your business on a weekly or monthly basis. Today the terms twitter, myspace, and facebook are all household names. Many businesses have been using these networking sites to maintain contact with their customers for years. The ability for customers to have a relationship with a business strengthens the bond and increases customer loyalty. Owning a web site allows you to link from the social networking sites to your business web site. Online marketing can involve just a web site, or it can use combinations of options. Social networking sites, blogs, web sites, advertisements both on and offline can all intertwine to make a strong business foundation.

Search engine optimization is the way to manipulate how a search engine views your web site. These methods of improvement lead to better visibility by the search engines and increase web site rank in the searches. The higher a site ranks the more visitors or traffic it obtains. It is the increase in traffic that offers more business leads and sales. Building a web site is just part of the process of creating your online presence. A web site must be found and read to be useful to a business or a customer. It is kind of like the example of a business that doesn't use a web site in comparison to one who does. Suppose the business that is online has an increase of 20% to their bottom line over the one that doesn't. If there are two competing businesses online of equal quality in products, customer service, and value, who will obtain more customers? The one with the higher web site ranking usually has the first opportunity to get a new customer, because it is found first. They have the first opportunity to build a relationship with the customer. This is where the value of having search engine optimization starts to become important.

Having a web site that isn't properly optimized is similar to having a ten-word advertisement without a business name or phone number in the country's largest newspaper. It will not generate sales leads and probably will not be read by most of the papers subscribers. A successful site needs to be visible to the search engines and to the customers. If you have an existing site, or are building one, an S.E.O. consultant can help you achieve your objectives for the web site. Consultants can provide an evaluation of your site and make recommendations, and or the necessary changes. A lot of web designers claim to have S.E.O. abilities but you need to be sure they do. Ask for examples of competitive key words that they currently rank for. If all they can rank for are six or eight word strings, they probably aren't very good. However, if they rank for two or three word competitive terms, then they probably have a clue.

Using Technology

Having established that customer relationships can help our business, what can we do to improve upon those bonds aside from the face-to-face approach that is a key to any business? Some of the new technologies that can help us stay in contact with customers and keep them involved are the social media avenues. Most people are familiar with the terms email, web site, Facebook, twitter and blogging. These things can help aid in creating customer contact, and business promotion. While these things may seem overwhelming to some, or not necessary by others, it is worth taking the time to see if these tools can help your business. You may come to the conclusion that maybe these things are not right for you, or your business. The possibility that these tools can help your business is also a realistic one as well. The important thing here is to find a method to stay in contact with your customers on a regular basis.

In today's world most businesses use the Internet to maintain some sort of online presence. Why would they do that? Well most customers today have Internet access or they know someone who does. A lot of customers now use the Internet in part of their decision-making when they purchase products. They use the Internet to find out about a specific product, where it can be purchased locally, compare it with competitor products, check for the best price, how to use a product and use this information to make a decision. Perhaps they wish to try something new and are seeking a local supplier, but they do not know where to find that product. The Internet is one of the most commonly used tools today so it only makes sense to have a web presence if you are in business.

When you are working with your customers, having a web site allows them to have a way to look up your latest or current promotions, and stay informed about you. When selling your products be sure the customer knows your web site address. Creating a customer list is another valuable tool to use for creating that connection. Having such a list will allow you to keep in touch with the customer, and also let you offer them promotions and sales in a fast effective manner. A web site may also be combined with a blog. The web site may offer information about the business, while the blog portion may offer frequent updates, and information.

Blogs for business are also a method of keeping customers in touch with your business. By informing your customers of your web site, they can look for your updates online. This may be conducted through a static web site, web site/blog combination, or a stand-alone blog. All have their specific uses and advantages. Blogs are often updated on a regular basis of some type, whether daily, weekly, monthly etc. These updates can vary by the users needs. A blog usually contains recent news or updates consistent with the writers interests. For example, a farmer may use a blog to keep his customers and readers informed about the progress of product development. They can follow along throughout the growth cycle and learn when it will be ready to harvest and go to market. The readers sometimes develop a personal connection through reading the posts, thus creating a stronger relationship between the customer and business owner. Often photos, video, and pod casts can be integrated into the blog allowing a great interactive environment for the reader. Blogs usually have the ability to allow readers to get current update alerts, and connect to twitter and Facebook as well. Blogging can be a valuable marketing tool in addition to a web site.

The ever-popular social networking sites twitter and Facebook are popular among businesses. Both of these allow the users to follow along with a user, staying up to date on the latest news. Twitter is sort of a micro blog, using short messages of 140 characters or less. Friends or followers receive updates as the user posts them. This provides a fast easy way of communicating with customers. Facebook is also an extremely popular method of networking. It allows customers and friends alike to keep up to date with more detailed messages and posts from a user. The network allows users to stay connected and send and receive messages. It allows more in depth communication, linking to blogs, web sites etc. Twitter also allows users to send a link but remember they only use 140 character messages.

These sites allow a user to stay in touch with friends and followers with minimal effort. Even for those who are not technically oriented, these options can assist in effective marketing. It is through communications like these that customers can stay in contact with a business. Maintaining regular contact helps keep the customer informed about what is going on with the business.   Building a personal relationship between the customer and business is important in any industry.

Develop a Customer List

Creating a list or database of customers is a very important part of marketing. The list allows you to keep track of your current customers, and allows you to market to them in the future. The value of a customer list is invaluable to your business. It gives you the ability to market to your customers over and over for years. It will allow you to gain customer feedback and test new products. With a good list the possibilities are endless, so a customer database is a valuable asset.

You should start building your list as soon as you start doing business. If you are already in business but do not have a list, start today. Make an effort to collect the names of your customers at every opportunity. It is easier than you think.

When you are selling your products put out a sign up sheet and be sure to ask each customer to sign up. You want to collect their name, address, email address and phone number if they will provide it. People are used to signing up for things so many will be more than happy to do so.

If you find your list is full of your current customers, or you are just starting out and want to create a list more quickly there are a few other methods you can try. You may want to do a drawing of some type, where perhaps you give away a sampling of your product or products. Everyone likes to win things. You may have people sign up that you currently are not doing business with and it may work for lead generation. Having extra people stop by your booth or retail location offers them an opportunity to see your products, talk to you and also perhaps sample your goods. That will allow you a potential chance to sell them your products.

Another method that can help you create your list is to offer a discount to those who sign up. If your customers already on the list want to refer a friend offer then a discount for that too. It is a great way to gain exposure and put more of your product on the market. Often a satisfied customer will be happy to give you a recommendation.

If you have a web site you can offer a sign up list on the site. This will allow people who already purchase from you, or those who are interested, to sign up online. Most people have an email address, and they may want to be notified by email. If you build a list of email addresses you can email your current specials or offerings to them all at once. The Internet is a terrific selling tool for any business, whether you sell products online or not.

You can use a newsletter to get customers to sign up with you. This allows you to build your list, and the newsletter offers you an opportunity to stay in contact with your customers. Your newsletter can be done by email, or print. Just be sure you can factor in the cost or be creative about getting it to the customer. The newsletter is an excellent opportunity to let your customers know about your business, products that are available, or ones that will be available soon. It is a great way to maintain contact with the customer. Maintaining a relationship with your customers on a regular basis will keep them interested, even in the off-season.

Now that you have a customer list, what can you do with it? As we have mentioned, it is important to stay in contact with your customers. The list can be used to get feedback about products and customer service. It can be used to tell customers about product availability, inform them about sales or future sales, inquire about other products they may be interested in, and to inform them about your business news. Customers can be very loyal if they like the products and are treated right. Making them feel important and keeping them informed about the business will help create a strong personal connection.

While owning a customer list is important, it is just as important not to abuse your list.

While it is important to keep contact with your customers, don't make the mistake of contacting them excessively. People quickly grow tired of high pressure or constant emails that are meaningless. You want to only contact your customers when you have something to share with them. Used responsibly, a good list will offer a lot of value to you. Used improperly, your list will cost you customers. A good rule of thumb is to contact your customers between 12 and 18 times a year. In other words, contact them one to one and a half times per month. As long as you are offering something of value every time you contact them, you will strengthen your relationship. Examples of valuable content include information about upcoming events and sales; discount coupons, information that the customer can use to improve their lives and tips about how to use your products.

Placing and Selling Your Farm Products

If you already have your product, either grown or created by your business, you are probably looking for places to sell it. If you are in the planning stages, it is good to consider where you will sell your product before it is ready for market. This is where planning helps you have a solid foundation for your business. Realistically you want to have your market before you have your product. This will enable you to plan how much to produce and at what intervals it will be ready to sell. Having a good marketing plan is important to any business.

If you are already selling your product, where are you selling it? How much of the product or products are you selling? Do you find yourself with more products than you can sell with your existing methods? Perhaps you are ready to expand to a larger venue to increase your profits. If you are already using the Internet, farmers markets, and off the farm sales, then you might be considering going to the retail stores. These opportunities often allow more people to see your product and the possibility to move more volume.

What kind of packaging will you be using for your products? This can vary greatly depending upon the type of product you have. Some products don't need packaging, while others may require being sealed and labeled with the ingredients that are in the product. You need to be sure you are in compliance with the local, state, and federal regulations for your products.

What sizes will you sell your products in if they are not sold by the piece? Will you need to put a weight somewhere on the packaging? If it is sold by the container what size will it be? U.P.C. codes or bar codes are used in many retail locations today. Whether you need one or not is something you need to determine. Depending upon your product and selling location you may or may not need it. The answer to this may come as you talk to potential clients about your products, labels and packaging. Some clients will welcome what you have; others may have very strict requirements. It is up to you to determine if it is cost effective, or if you will do enough business to make special arrangements for one or two accounts. Sometimes it is very beneficial, other times it may just not be cost effective to have that business relationship. So you need to know what is required, and also what you can afford to do.

Pricing Your Products

While this is not exactly related to getting your product into a retail store it is important. Determining your price is something that you should have already done from the time you started selling. There are many factors that go into determining your price for an item. Each individual business will have different input costs for the same type of product. This means you have to factor in your cost for everything that you do related to producing and marketing that product. Tracking is essential for everything that you do in business. This information can be used to help you determine your costs, profits and price adjustments within the business.

When you start to calculate your pricing, take into consideration where you will sell the intended product. Are you going to retail the product yourself? Is the product going to be sold to a retail location or to a distributor? Obviously if the product is going to a middleman they are not going to pay a retail price for the product, as they must also make a profit. This is why it is important to know your input costs and your breakeven price. You need to know exactly to the penny if possible what you have invested in your product and getting it to market. At that point you can begin to determine your profit per item at different price levels. Do not make the mistake of guessing at your costs, or thinking that you can figure it out later. Don't fall into the trap of following another businesses pricing either. Remember everyone has their individual input costs; in turn everyone will have different profit margins.

After you have determined your pricing, decide how much product you have to sell. This will help you determine some potential outlets for your products. You may very well need to know the answer to that question when you start talking to a store or distributor. They need to know how much product you will have available and for how long a time period. Obviously there is a difference in having a year round product and a seasonal one. How much will be available at one time, and how much will they need? Each potential customer may have different needs. So you need to know exactly what you can provide before approaching a potential account.

After determining your pricing structures, what you can supply to a customer and at what intervals, it is time to start working on prospective clients. Make a list of potential accounts that would have a need for your product. You might also want to make a list of people in your personal network that may be of help to you. Can they or someone they know offer you any assistance? Who do they know in their network that might offer a hand? Networking plays a big role in business and should not be overlooked. After reviewing your lists it is now time to start contacting your potential clients.

One of the most important decisions in running your business is setting price. In order to be in business and sell goods or services you have to have a price that allows you to operate profitably. What is price? A price is a perceived value for goods or services. There are many factors that can go into calculating your prices. It is important to know exactly what your costs are because you need to know as much as possible about your input costs to help set your price. This is where tracking comes into play, it will give you effective information to use in your decision making process.

What kind of price are you calculating? This is important to know before you start. Are you creating a price for retail? Are you creating a wholesale price? Certainly they are two different prices, with two different purposes. A wholesale client will not pay you retail prices for your product because they cannot make a profit. On the other hand you cannot afford to sell wholesale to your retail customers because you will be minimizing your profit potential. You need to set the price according to what you intend to do with the product. You will need to create both prices, a wholesale and retail price, if you intend to sell to both markets.

When setting or creating prices a few other factors to take into consideration are what type of prices you are creating. Are you creating temporary pricing? These types of prices are for entry into a market, sales, clearing inventory, or survival so they are specific purposed prices for the short term. Having a short-term price strategy may or may not be a part of your business but it if is, determine the effects it may have on the business before you do so. Long-term price strategies are important for the survival of your business so take that into consideration when setting your prices and creating your plan.

What is the market demand for your product? How much of the market share do you have within the area you are selling? If you control a large portion of the market with your products obviously it's a little easier to set and control price. What kind of demand is there for your product or service? Do you offer a unique product or service? Customers will likely pay more for products that are unique or harder to obtain.

There are many factors that go into creating a price structure. The prices you set will be determined by your individual situation. Every business is different in costs, goals, product demand, desired mark up, and desired profits so carefully evaluate when setting your prices.

Your total costs will play a large role in your pricing decisions. If you have tracked as much as possible about your business costs it will help you make a more informed choice. You will have both fixed costs and variable costs to consider in your price. Your fixed costs are always constant and are not subject to quick changes. Variable costs are not consistent and may change from month to month or day to day, seasonally, or by each shipment or cycle. Tracking these costs leads to a more efficient total cost of goods. Using a real total expense number will allow you to achieve your breakeven point and also calculate a real price for profit.

Having historical data from the past year will help you in making decisions for the next years pricing. Looking at the prior years fixed costs will help you gain a picture of the next year. The variable costs will be tied to production, wages, fuel, shipping costs, materials etc. that may change more rapidly. These numbers can be used to estimate your costs.

Previously we had mentioned market demand. It plays an important role in determining price on a product. What is the demand for your product? What is the projected market supply for similar products? Do you control a large share of the market? Whether you are in the off-season or peak season for a product may affect the price you are able to charge. What competitor products are available and in what quantities? Price is sometimes referred to as the maximum price a customer will pay or the price the market will bear. Knowing your demand will help you set price. Usually price and demand are inversely related; the lower the price the higher the demand, the higher the price the lower the demand. Your price should be somewhere between your cost and what the market will bear. Pricing should be set at such a level that is creates a fair profit and is also fair to your customers. Consumer income also plays a role in supply and demand, as income rises so does demand, as income falls demand also decreases.

How does the customer perceive your product? How your product is viewed plays a role in the maximum price a customer will pay. What is the customer's view of your product? It can be helpful to put yourself in your customer's shoes. The perceived customer value should offer you an ability to make a profit, or you may need to rethink some of your strategies. What are similar competitors prices? Compare your product or service to what is being offered, and compare similar features. This may help you in setting your price. What would you pay for your product if you were the customer? Prices can be too high or too low and both will have adverse effects on your ability to sell.

Talking To Potential Accounts

Try to learn as much as possible about the accounts you are interested in doing business with. Do you know of any other business that may sell to that account? Talk to them about their business relationship if they will. You may learn a lot about what is required and how things work with that particular retail or wholesale client from someone already selling to them. It is very important to find out who the buyer is, or the person who is in charge of making the buying decisions. The job title may vary from place to place, but somewhere there is a person who is in charge of purchasing. It is your job to find out who the person is and contact them to set up your appointment.

If you are having trouble finding out who to talk to, stop into the location and talk to one of the employees, especially in the department you might be selling your product from. If you can't find who you need, ask a sales associate or cashier for assistance. Most people are very friendly and will help guide you to the right person. Once you determine who the buyer is, try to obtain an appointment with them.

Depending upon the type of store or distributor, they may have information online about their store. Some businesses will list their requirements for vendors on their web site. Each business may be different on requirements for presentation of new products for consideration. Large chain stores will obviously have different requirements than the locally owned grocery store. Do not let that discourage you! You just need to find out what you need to do, and get it done. If there are specific guidelines be sure to follow it completely or they may not give you consideration. Remember that a lot of companies get offered new products on a regular basis, so try to have everything as complete as possible.

When you are able to meet with the potential account, be sure to create and practice a nice presentation for your product. Remember you are doing the selling, having a good product is part of it but you are also selling the customer on yourself. How you present yourself and your product will reflect on their perception of your business. If you go into a meeting with a nice product display and good literature and samples it goes a long ways toward establishing a business relationship. Practice your sales presentation until you are comfortable with it; know your products, and your business. Never go into a meeting unprepared, or put on a poor presentation that is just thrown together, and never be late! Everything you do in business reflects back to you. If you create a bad first impression it may reduce your chances of creating that important opportunity.

When you talk to the buyer, it is important to let them know what you or your product can do for their business. They are not there to help you out; they are in business to make a profit. It is up to you to convince them that you have a product that will help them. It is about what you can offer and how it will improve what they are doing for their customers. So determine what your strong points are about your products and your business and be sure to point that out. If you offer something unique, or have a special process or method be sure to let them know. The meeting is your opportunity to present the products and business at its best.

The presentation may lead to questions about what products you can provide, how much volume you have to offer and how often you will have it. Try to have the answers to common questions pertaining to your products. They may want to make changes to your sizing etc. Is that something you are open to doing? Is it even affordable to consider making changes of that nature? Sometimes it is, and sometimes it may not be cost effective. Other times it is negotiable, and they might want things a certain way but will go along with the product the way it is. You have to be willing to talk to the buyers and find out exactly what is required of you, and also what to expect from them.

You will probably talk about pricing, which is why you need to have determined your costs and price structure before selling or meeting anyone about product. Another thing that you need to consider is terms of payment. When will you get paid? How will you get paid? You may find a few accounts that pay on delivery, however most companies tend to want to pay 15 days, 30 days, 45 days, or 60 days later. You need to decide what you can afford to do first. How much product can you front without getting paid? Can you even afford to work with those terms of payment? You may be able to negotiate a short term of payment, but perhaps not. You definitely need to ask yourself these questions and also be willing to talk it over with the buyer when the time comes.

You should also be able to work out a schedule for delivery of your product. You want to make sure you deliver exactly what is ordered, and at the appropriate time, and in the necessary packaging. How will the product be handled when you arrive? Do you need it on a pallet? Will you have it in boxes where they will break it down at a later time? You want things to be as exact as possible, and also as simple as possible for both you and the store. How you deliver your product and interact in your business relationship is just as important as the quality of your goods. Gaining an account is just part of process, you also want to maintain that good relationship for the future.

Tracking Everything In Your Business

An important task in business is tracking. You need to track everything that you do in order to know the status of your business. Keeping good records and data is essential for any business. If you have a good tracking system in place you will know more about your business, and be able to make sound effective decisions in the future.

What should you track? You should track everything from your input costs to your sales and everything in between. You need this data to determine how profitable you actually are, to help you determine your break even points, set your prices, choose advertising and much more. The more you start to use this information the more valuable it will become to you when making cost effective and profit making decisions. Using actual data to make choices rather than guessing will lead to more profitable outcomes.

The first step would be to track all of your costs. To really do this right you need to track each thing you do separately. If you are raising 10 different types of produce how much do you have in each one? What does it cost to raise that head of lettuce or blueberry? Keeping detailed records is vital. What does it cost to plant, raise, and harvest and sell that crop? You need to factor in all costs including labor. Doing this will give you a true accounting of what you have in each item. If you have a true number of your input cost, you know what your break-even point is.

You need to know what it costs to market your products. How much do you spend a year on advertising? Do you know which ads are generating sales and which ones are not? If you run multiple ads and use different methods of advertising you need to know which ones are working. Advertising is expensive so you need to know that every effort you make to sell your product yields results. You can do this by tracking your ads. It is important to know what it costs to sell, and also what it costs to gain a new customer.

If you are running advertisements, assign a promotional code or number to the coupon. When the customers call in or present the coupon with the order or purchase the code will allow you to determine where it came from. It is really important to know where your sales are coming from. By using codes or numbers with your promotions you will be able to start tracking your results more effectively. Once you determine the source of your sales, you can reduce or eliminate the ads that are not as effective. The more effective your marketing, the lower your customer cost. This in turn offers you more profit potential and less wasted time.

You should be tracking all of your marketing efforts. What does it cost to deliver your products? What does it cost to travel to a farmers market or other selling venue? If you sell at multiple locations, what are your costs and sales from each?

Rather than looking at just the big picture of total inputs and total sales you also should evaluate individual products and venues. This will offer you a better picture of your profits, costs, and losses for each item you sell.

If you are raising different varieties of produce and you track each one completely you will know what is profitable and what is not. Perhaps you are growing a crop that offers little profits but you are unaware because a more profitable crop is covering the costs. The big picture looks nice because you are making profit, even though you don't realize that one crop is carrying another. You will discover this with proper tracking and at that point you might decide you would be better off raising a greater amount of the profitable variety thus increasing your bottom line.

How much of your business comes from your web site? If you are selling only online then you probably know the answer to that question. You may know the answer anyway. If you are selling at multiple locations, and also online then all you may be looking at are the total sales and total costs. You can track your online orders. It is important to know where your sales and sales leads come from. This will allow you to focus on improving your marketing plan.

Web site traffic can also be tracked with special software. You can learn what your visitors were searching for when they used a search engine, which search engine they were using, what page they entered your site on, what page they left on and how long they stayed on each page. These statistics can be used to help you better understand your customers and also evaluate your online business. Are your customers finding you from natural traffic from the search engines? Are they finding you from links? Do you use banner advertising or online classifieds? Does the traffic to your site come from your social networking profiles? It is important to know as much about your customer base as possible. This will allow you to be more effective with your advertising budget.

How much inventory do you have? What did the inventory cost you to produce, buy, or build? Do you know how much you sell daily, weekly or monthly? What does it cost you to store these items? Inventory can tie up a lot of your capital depending on your type of business. It is important to keep a proper balance, know exactly what you have on hand, and know exactly what the cost of storage is.

Do you track your time? How much work do you do on a daily basis? Time is not free even if you own your own business so track it accordingly. If you hire employees how much time do they put in? Let's break it down further; how much time is invested in labor for each individual product? This is part of your cost per item even though you have the employee hired for a day at a certain wage per hour. Figuring your cost per item can help with time management decisions and production choices if you must reduce or increase volumes. The more you know about what you spend and where you are spending it the easier it is to make educated choices.

Anything that you do with your business needs to be tracked. It is important to know exactly what your costs are for each product or service you offer. It is easy to fall into the thought of I will do it later, or I will add that cost later and forget. It is important to keep accurate records that will allow you to determine piece by piece what you have invested in your products. This will allow you to determine your profits or losses. When it comes time to reduce costs you want to be able to cut costs in the proper areas. This is why tracking is so important.

How can you determine price, or break-even points without knowing your true cost? If you have the necessary data to calculate your costs, it is much easier to calculate your price and make effective decisions. Tracking will allow you to determine how much profit your business is really making. Without tracking every detail of your operation it is hard to determine profitability as a whole or on a per item basis.

General Marketing

To close out this book I decided to include a general marketing overview that I put together a while back for a different purpose. I didn't end up using it at the time but it came to mind while editing this book. It covers some of the same thing you have already read here, but it also adds some important concepts that can help your business.

This is not a traditional marketing plan. There are different sections below that can be used individually or in combination to form a plan. The marketing sections are separated into online and offline, and this is not an exhaustive list.

Online Marketing

Search Engine Optimization (SEO) – SEO is the process of making a web site rank higher in the popular search engines (Google, Yahoo and MSN) to increase the traffic to the site. There are many different things that SEO covers, but included here are the most important.

Every page should have a unique title and description and include the main keyword phrase in an H1 tag. Secondary keyword phrases can also be included in an H2 tag. Every page on the site should be linked to from at least 5 other pages on the same site using the main keyword phrase, or derivative of the main keyword phrase, as anchor text of the link. For example, if the page being linked to is about seed potatoes, the link to that page should say seed potatoes. Each page should also have a minimum of 200 words about the subject of the page, and 500 or more words of content per page is better.

A list of terms that you wish to rank for should be compiled and a page should be added to the web site about each of these terms. Terms that are similar can be covered on the same page, but targeting more than 3 or 4 keyword phrases per page is not a good idea.

Links from other web sites and quality directories (DMOZ, Yahoo, etc) also help your site rank better in the search engines. You can also write or have written articles and submit them to the large article directories to get links back to the site. You can also find other web site owners that will let you write an article for their site and provide a link back to your site from within the article.

Pay Per Click (PPC) – PPC marketing is paying for clicks to your site from small advertisements placed along with normal search results. Google and Yahoo are the 2 best PPC companies and provide the best traffic. PPC can be expensive and all results need to be tracked so you make sure your best keywords are used more and the lower quality ones are canceled.

Affiliate Marketing – You can set up an affiliate program where people that already have traffic to their web sites can send traffic to you and you pay a percentage of the sale to them for the traffic. You may also pay a flat fee per sale instead of a percentage.

Flat Ad Space Buys – You may buy ad space, either banner ads, reviews or just links to your site from other web sites that have traffic that may be interested in your offers.

Offline Marketing

Write a Book – By authoring a book on your subject you will be an instant expert to many people. The book does not have to be published by a traditional publishing house. It can be self-published using an online service like CreateSpace (owned by Amazon). The most important thing is to make sure the book is available for order on Amazon.com as many prospective customers will check if it is available there.

Magazine Articles – Having articles published in magazines also builds expert status within your target market. Getting magazine articles published is not hard as long as you can write well or have articles written well for you. Not every magazine you target will publish your material, but if you are persistent you will get into print.

Interviews – Find media outlets that already reach your target market and determine how to be interviewed by that media. The book and magazine articles listed above help you get interviewed as well. You can also seek out Internet based sites, radio and television programs that are usually much more open to interviews than traditional off line media.

Press Releases – A press release can achieve a high level of free publicity if it draws interest from media outlets. There are many press release services available online that distribute to online and off line media. Media is always looking for information to fill their schedule but it is important that your press release be viewed as newsworthy.

Direct Mail – You can rent lists of potential customers based on things they have bought in the past or magazines they are subscribed to. This is a way to narrow down prospective customers and reach them directly. It is important to track all responses to direct mail, as it can be expensive if you don't work it correctly. It is difficult to sell a high priced offer on the front end in direct mail, so you should craft an offer that gets them into your marketing funnel and shows the prospective customer that you offer a quality service/product. It is often worth creating a lower level information product that you can sell for a low cost just to get customers who you can then market higher priced products and services to.

House List – Every contact and customer needs to be kept on your house list. This can include an email list as well as a direct mail list. Customers that already are in your marketing funnel are much more likely to buy from you again, and most of the things you do in regards to marketing should be with an eye on increasing the size of your house list.

Consulting, Speaking, Services and Training Opportunities

Consulting, speaking, training and services are available for a wide range of businesses. Here is just a small sampling of things that I do. If you think I may be able to help you make more money, please see the next chapter to learn how to contact me.

Consulting:

Marketing
Profitability
Internet sales and transition
Inventory management
Pricing strategies
Customer service
Direct mail
Advertising
Copywriting

Speaking:

> Short, medium and long programs from sales meetings and dinner engagements to multi-day conferences.

Services:

> Marketing plan creation
> Web site design
> Search engine optimization (SEO)
> Complete marketing solutions
> Web site management
> Newsletter creation
> Content generation

Training:

> Marketing
> Sales
> Retail
> Service
> SEO
> Web site

About The Authors

The reason I am going to tell you about my past experiences in marketing and business is not to brag, but to show you that I have used in the real world what I am telling you works. I have read too many books that were obviously written by someone who hasn't actually used their own advice in a real business. Of course you don't have to believe that my ideas work, you just need to try them. The only way that you won't profit from the information included in this book is if you don't read it or don't use it after you have read it. These marketing tactics work and you will be able to see it for yourself once you get started. I urge you to put a few of the ideas into action and see the results for yourself before just assuming something won't work. You will be pleasantly surprised, I assure you.

For over 20 years I have been running, buying, selling, creating and consulting with businesses of every shape and size. My experience runs from working with businesses doing less than $100,000 in yearly sales to businesses doing over $1 Billion in annual revenues. (Yes, that is Billion with a B). My marketing background includes work with all types of advertising including magazines, newspapers, radio, television and direct mail as well as using social media, e-mail and the Internet. It also includes all of the other things that aren't advertising that are included in marketing. These don't need to be listed here because you are getting ready to learn more about them in this book.

Here is an example of what I have done for businesses that I have been involved with. This is an actual business and the numbers are real, but I am not going to disclose the name of the business to protect them from their competitors. It is a fairly typical retail business. When I started working with them, their yearly sales were just under $1.5 Million with a gross profit of 22%. The big problem was that they were running around 22% of sales as expenses also. If you have been in business long at all you realize that 22% going out and 22% coming in leaves nothing in the profit column. This is also a recipe for disaster because if your cash flow falters you don't have any cushion.

Within two years the business had improved sales to just under $3 Million, improved their gross profit to over 30% and were keeping their expenses at 25% of sales. Not only were we able to double sales, we were also able to create a 5% spread between gross profit and expense percentage. This created a 5% margin in the net profit before taxes column. This is what I do. Create profits that go directly to the bottom line.

Many prospective clients and other people who I talk to that are interested in my services and what I do ask me about my educational background. While I am educated in the business world, holding a Masters degree in Business Administration, I always stress that my real education has come by actually working in a business and learning what works and what doesn't first hand. Most of what I learned in school has not been valuable in the real world. The good thing is I have both areas covered. If a business will only work with an "educated" individual, I fit the bill. On the other hand, if a business is only worried about dealing with a person that has actually made money in the trenches, I fit that bill too. My plan was to cover as many bases as possible. This should be the plan in your business as well.

Other experiences that have helped me prepare to help businesses of all types and size include teaching occasional business courses at the college level, speaking to groups of business people, writing for different business markets and working as a co-host on a business radio show.

You will find many ways to help your business and increase your profits in this book. But if you feel that my services can help you even more, there is information at the back of the book about how to contact me.

My friend, business associate and occasional business partner Rich Vance has also contributed to this book. Here is some additional information about his business experience and background.

He has many years of experience in the business world working with both online and offline marketing. Rich has been heavily involved in the agricultural business for over 20 years, using traditional and non-traditional methods of marketing. He also has experience in the automotive industry with sales and management experience and has worked with retail and commercial accounts with a major retailer.

The past four years he has been working extensively in online marketing and search engine optimization (SEO). Whether working with a start up business or existing business, there are always ways to improve marketing, management or sales practices and his experience allows him to effectively help whichever type of business is in need.

Contact information for Rich Vance can be found at the end of this book.

How To Contact The Authors

If you have comments about the book, are looking for a speaker for your next business event or are interested in any of the services offered by the author, you can contact me by mail at the following address or by email. Correspondence for Rich Vance can also be sent to the same address.

Wesley R. Young
PO Box 10
Middleport, OH 45760

info@ranchandfarmmarketingguide.com

If you wish to speak about working with me by phone, include detailed information about your business, what you are interested in, your phone number and the best times to reach you.

Notes

Notes

Notes